10 minute CRAFTS for WINTER

ANNALEES LIM

First published in 2013 by Wayland
Copyright © Wayland 2013

Wayland
338 Euston Road
London NW1 3BH

Wayland Australia
Hachette Children's Books
Level 17/207
Kent Street
Sydney, NSW 2000

Senior Editor: Julia Adams
Craft stylist: Annalees Lim
Designer: Emma Randall
Photographer: Simon Pask, N1 Studios

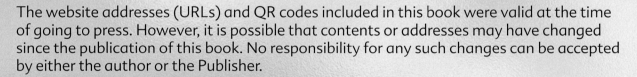

A CIP catalogue record for this book is available from the British Library.

ISBN 978 0 7502 7773 0

Printed in China

Wayland is a division of Hachette Children's Books,
an Hachette UK company.

www.hachette.co.uk

Picture acknowledgements:
All step-by-step craft photography: Simon Pask, N1 Studios;
images used throughout for creative graphics: Shutterstock

Contents

WINTER

Winter is one of the seasons of the year. The months of winter are December, January and February.

Winter is the coldest season of the year and has the smallest amount of daylight. Most winter trees are completely bare, as all their leaves have fallen to the ground during the autumn months. You are more likely to see hail, frost and even snow. But don't let that stop you from going outside and enjoying the winter landscape.

Snow is just one of the fun things about winter. You can build snowmen, go sledging and even make snow angels. Winter might be cold, with all of the animals snuggled up and hibernating, but there is still loads to do and see!

This book will guide you to all the great natural materials you can collect. Bring them back home and discover what great craft projects you can make in the comfort of your warm home.

Whatever you find, remember to always ask a grown up before you pick it up. A good rule to remember is to only collect what has fallen from plants or trees and never pick anything that is still alive or growing. Always remember to wash your findings before you use them.

Mini pine forest

One of the only trees to stay green all through the winter is the pine tree. It has needles instead of leaves. Make your own mini pine forest using cuttings from larger trees.

You will need:

- Pine tree cuttings
- Modelling clay
- Plastic pot lid
- PVA glue
- Paintbrush
- Flour
- Brown, yellow and red card
- Scissors
- Pencil

1

Press down some modelling clay in a plastic lid.

If you can't find any pine tree cuttings, you can use some twigs, making it look like a lovely, bare, wintery forest.

2

Lightly coat each pine cutting with some PVA glue. Sprinkle some flour over the glue and shake the excess off.

6

3 Press the pine cuttings into the modelling clay.

4 Fold a piece of coloured card in half and cut out a tear drop shape.

5 Keep the paper folded and make a small cut at the top to make the wings. Draw the bird's details using a pencil. Decorate your trees with lots of coloured birds.

Bird bingo

If you are quiet and still, you can spot lots of different breeds of birds. You can turn your bird spotting into a game of bingo. Just cover the bird you have spotted with a counter and when you have spotted all the birds on your card, just shout BINGO! Only don't shout too loudly or you will scare the birds away.

You will need:
- Paper
- Ruler
- coloured pens or pencils
- coloured card
- Scissors

Fold your piece of paper to create six sections. Draw the dividing lines using a pen and a ruler.

Draw one bird into each of the six sections.

3 Colour in the birds using coloured pencils.

4 Make some counters by cutting six squares of coloured card that fit on the bird squares.

Not all birds stay with us throughout the winter, so check before you draw them on your card. We have included a robin, a sparrow, a dove, a blue tit, a chaffinch and a blackbird on our bingo card.

Twirling twig hanging

Nature is often quite bare in the winter. Why not try this craft to brighten up your garden or even your room. Use twigs you have collected from a wintery walk and decorate your hanging with shiny beads.

You will need:
- Twigs
- String
- Beads
- Scissors

1 Choose four short twigs, four medium twigs and four long ones.

2 Make three squares by tying each of the four twigs of the same length together at each corner.

3

Tie all three squares together using one long piece of string.

4

Thread beads onto short pieces of string and attach them to the squares.

5

Tie a loop of string to the top of your hanging, and hang it up in the garden or your room.

Watch this video to find out how to make a hanging star!

11

Bird feeder

It is harder for birds to find food and keep warm in the winter. You can help by making this simple bird feeder using a pine cone you have collected on one of your walks.

You will need:
- Pine cone
- Lard
- Bird seed
- String
- Scissors
- Plate
- Butter knife

1 Tie some string around the top of the pine cone.

2 Press the lard into the pine cone using a butter knife.

3

Put your bird seed onto a plate.

4

Roll the pine cone in the seed mix to cover it evenly.

There are many different types of bird feeders you can make. Look out for more designs so you can feed as many birds as possible.

13

Sticks and stones

You may be tempted to stay inside during winter, but you'll be surprised how much fun you can have in the frost and snow! This simple and fun game can be made and played when you venture outside.

You will need:
- sticks
- stones
- string
- scissors
- correction fluid

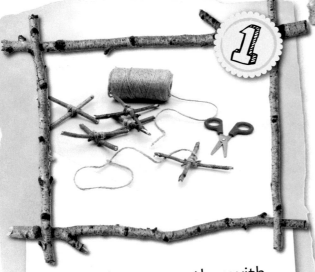

Tie two twigs together with string, in the shape of a cross. Make five of these in total.

Find five large, flat stones and draw a large circle on each of them with correction fluid.

3

Make the grid using the four long sticks.

4

Use correction fluid to draw a circle on one side of a stone, and a line on the other side.

How to play:
This is a simple game of noughts and crosses. Use the stone with the circle and line to flip and see who goes first. Noughts use the stones and crossed uses the sticks.

Scented hanging

Winter has its own smells and scents. When you are outside, notice how crisp frosty mornings or pine forests smell. But it's not just the outdoors – some fruit and spices remind us of winter, too. This simple hanging craft will spread a lovely wintry scent in your home.

You will need:

- Ribbon
- Slice of dried orange
- cloves
- cinnamon stick
- Sprig of holly
- craft glue
- scissors
- Three red beads

1 Tie a long piece of ribbon through the slice of the dried orange.

2 Press some cloves into the orange slice.

3 Tie a cinnamon stick to the top of the orange slice using the ribbon.

4 Using craft glue, stick two holly leaves and the red beads onto the cinnamon sticks.

5 Tie the ribbon into a bow, so you can hang it up.

Dry your own orange by cutting it onto slices about 1cm thick and cooking the slices in the oven at 120 degrees for 2-3 hours, turning occasionally.

Ice mobiles

Winter is usually very cold and some nights it can be below zero degrees. Make the most of the freezing temperatures by making a really cool ice sculpture that you can hang outside!

You will need:

- Plastic container
- String
- Pebbles
- Sticks
- Aniseed star
- Scissors

1 In a plastic container, make a pattern out of some pebbles, sticks and an aniseed star.

Try using unusual jelly moulds to create fun shapes for your ice mobiles.

2 Tie a knot in a length of string and place it in the plastic container. You may want to secure it in place with sticky tape.

3

Fill the plastic container with water, so it covers the pebbles.

4

Put the container in the freezer until it has frozen. If it is a really cold night, you can try leaving it outside.

5

Take the ice block out of the container and hang it up outside.

Potato print snowman

Snow can melt really quickly when the sun starts to shine again. Make it last a little longer by making a printed snowman with potatoes and twigs you have gathered.

You will need:

- Potato
- White, brown, orange and black paint
- Blue card
- Plate or paint pallet
- Twigs
- Pencil

1

Ask an adult to cut a potato in half.

2

Spread white paint on the cut surface of each potato half. Use the halves to print the head and body of the snowman.

Use twigs to print some arms with brown paint.

Using some black paint, use the top and bottom side of a pencil to print the face.

Spread some orange paint on a small stick to print the nose. You can use your fingertip and some white paint to print snow.

Follow this link to find out how to print fun shapes using cookie cutters!

Penguin skittles

Penguins live in the Arctic, where it's winter all year round! You can make your own feathered friends and play for hours with this fun skittles game.

1 Cut a strip of black card the height of the drink container. This will make the head and body of the penguin.

2 Fold the card in half and cut a 'B' shape out. Then wrap the card around the drink container and fasten it with sticky tape.

3 Cut two 'U' shapes out of black card to make wings. Glue them to the side of the penguin body.

4 Cut out orange feet and stick them to the bottom of the body. Glue on googly eyes.

5 Cut out two yellow triangles, fold them in half and stick them onto the head to form the beak. Make another nine penguins!

Follow this link to find out how to make robins for your skittles game!

23

Glossary

frost powdery ice that forms on things in freezing weather

gather to collect

hail pellets of frozen rain that fall in showers

hibernate when an animal goes to sleep for the winter

pine a tree that has needles instead of leaves and stays green in the winter; pine trees are used to celebrate Christmas

skittles a game that involves rolling a ball towards nine pins in order to knock as many of them down as possible

sledging to travel across the snow on a sledge; a sledge is a vehicle that has metal or wooden strips instead of wheels

Index

10 minute CRAFTS

Titles in the series:

AUTUMN
978 0 7502 7772 3

Pine cone squirrel
Apple hedgehog prints
Dried leaf bonfire
Field mouse
Spider web
Mini owls
Scarecrow
Book worm
Conker creatures

SUMMER
978 0 7502 7771 6

Crawling crabs
Butterfly pegs
Seascape in a bottle
Sandcastles
Flower prints
Mini kites
Sunflower pot
Rafts
Starfish

SPRING
978 0 7502 7774 7

Fluffy sheep
Life of a seed
Leaf print flowers
Daffodil paperweight
Bark rubbing
Bouncing bunnies
Twig hanging
Potted flowers
Soil picture

WINTER
978 0 7502 7773 0

Mini pine forest
Bird bingo
Twirling twig hanging
Bird feeder
Sticks and stones
Scented hanging
Ice mobile
Potato print snowman
Penguin skittles